IN
SEARCH
OF
A TITLE

~ Musings Of A Teenager

AASHNA LIDDER

Creative
CROWS
PUBLISHERS LLP
the publishing & communication people

Published by

Office: A-42, Dayanand Colony,
New Delhi(South)-110024
Emails: ganivpanjrath@yahoo.co.in, tannaazirani@gmail.com

Disclaimer

This book is a work of fiction and any resemblance to actual persons living or dead is
purely coincidental.

ISBN-13: 978-81-949782-6-8
ISBN 10: 81-949782-6-2
Book Size: 5.5*8.5

Printed and bound by Creative Crows Publishers LLP

To two things;
The zest for life and my grandmother,
For making my heart so full.

CONTENTS

If words could speak;
If prose could sing;
If phrases could flow;
If poetry could fly;
Then poets would spread,
Melodies from space,
through hills and dales,
to the earthmen below.

Aashna has encapsuled, the spirit of humanity through poems. Growing up in a military family, she has experienced the highs and lows every child in a situation like her has been through. Words and phrases are expression of her belief and there surely is a budding poet, waiting to be recognised. So continue your quest in poetry with passion and wish you the best.

(Bipin Rawat)
General
Chief of Defence Staff

25 August 2021

THE SHRI RAM SCHOOL

V-37, MOULSARI AVENUE. PHASE-III, DLF CITY, GURUGRAM. PHONE : 0124-4784400
E-mail address: senior.school@tsrs.org
D-3 STREET, VASANT VIHAR, NEW DELHI-110057. PHONE : 26140884, 26149572
E-mail address: junior.school@tsrs.org
Website: www.tsrs.org

Cambridge Assessment
International Education
Cambridge International School

1st September 2021

Aashna
As the name suggests stemming from the word hope
Hope and love, the two words that hold so much meaning;

Aashna
Your immense talent, to play with words
To string every bead into this pure pearly string;

Aashna
wisdom beyond years for someone all of sixteen
to express and emote like you have;

Aashna
Savouring your words
the bitter sweet words
Make me wonder how deep you are
Our shining star!

Go girl
Wear your soul on your sleeve
Create magical potions of love moods and words!
Dream big and may you always pursue your love for writing and creating sheer magic.

Thank you

Warm Regards,

Manika Sharma
मणिका शर्मा
Director
The Shri Ram Schools
Phone +91-124-4784404, Fax +91-124-4784439
EA to the Director Ms. Vandana Dargan: - Vandana.dargan@tsrs.org
website: www.tsrs.org
Vasant Vihar campus location: http://bit.ly/TSRS-VasantVihar
Moulsari campus location: http://bit.ly/TSRS-Moulsari
Aravali campus location: http://bit.ly/TSRS-Aravali

| Core Values : | Integrity | Sensitivity | Pursuit of excellence | Pride in one's own heritage |

An Initiative of SRF Limited

QSI International School of Zhuhai
1689 Yinwan Road - Wanzai, Zhuhai, China 51903
Tel. +86-756-815-6134 email: zhuhai.qsi.org

Director – Mr. Jay Loftin

To Whom it May Concern;

It is always an honor and a privilege to not only see the great talents in our students, but to see them before others do. Aashna Lidder, from the first day she burst on the scene, stole the stage, took the air out of the room in one big breath, and sang back life. I know that she will do great things, and has already begun. Her poems are moving and bittersweet; everything they should be.

The only constant is change. Throughout the human journey, there has been an ebb and flow in the very changing world that like a Shakespearean theme, is timeless and uninterrupted. The human experience. It is universal. It is always new and yet always repeating itself. And nothing has ever personified this journey like the voice of a young woman. Not just any voice can do this. It takes a special voice, one steeped in wisdom beyond her years, one connected to something itself timeless, one who knows she is a snapshot of God on this earth. Aashna is one such voice. It is her brokenness, her joy, her pain, her purity that makes every word holy and an offering of frailty. It is that vulnerability one can find in the writings of Aashna Lidder. This single clear note is a tone that vibrates the chords of the heart and reminds even the oldest ear what the song of youth was. It is music. It is pure. It is Aashna, completely.

Respectfully yours.

J.J.oftin

QSI INTERNATIONAL
SCHOOL OF ZHUHAI

Jay M. Loftin DIRECTOR

✉ 1689 Yinwan Road - Wanzai   ☎ +86-756-815-6134
   Zhuhai, China 51903   🌐 zhuhai.qsi.org

Jay Loftin

Brig R.S Duggal

Tele : 0172-778046
Mob : 9815395984

1057, Sector 8-C
Chandigarh-160001

THE BOMBAY SAPPERS

I have seen **Aashna** blossom into a fine young lady. I thought I knew her well till I read her '*musings*', a collection of thought provoking poems. Truly, I had to read them a couple of times to understand the large and depth of her emotions – now I began to understand her '*Adulting!*'

The young poetess has presented a colourful kaleidoscope of emotions, giving glimpse of her soul. Various shades and hues of feelings have made intricate designs of poetry – one design that holds the set of poems is '*Innocence to Adolescence*'! In her journey through schools, places and people she makes the reader a co-traveller.

She is just sixteen now but her personality is touching lives. She inspires by being a good student, a great debater and sports person of note. The poems besides touching the young are a must read for parents. These poems will make the parents reflect and understand the adolescent mind - with its apprehensions, relationships, joys, aspirations and more.

My very best wishes to Aashna-looking forward to more such creative joys.

Brig (Retd.) R.S. Duggal

(A loving and proud grandfather)

PROLOGUE

by

Geetika Lidder

Aashna is a very special baby to us, just as all babies are. She made us wait for her, pray for her and desire her with all that we had – for she came in after 8 years of our marriage, many prayers, Novinas, fasts, religious trips, pandit trips and so on... the entire jamboree one can experience when something so special evades you and you go into a "Why me?" downward spiralling tornado.

As such her name itself means "devoted/ devotion" and "friend". We have tried to raise her as our friend and we remain devoted and indebted to her with all our hearts for the happiness she brought us in our lives. We believe in our karmic connection and the faith that she and us have debts to repay to each other.

So, the journey of debts continues...as the child grows and the family experiences all the milestones, growing up pangs and pleasures specific to each age group, gender and stage.

My prelude is just my miniscule, humble expression of love and gratitude to all that is and will be – Aashna.

2004

The first image that comes to my mind

As I see you today

Is that tiny heart which was beating so fast

On that very special day

The ultrasound was loud and clear

For a petrified me to see

The tiny heart which was beating

Would very soon be our baby.

The journey to bring you home

Was never an easy one

It had all the trials and tribulations

And was nowhere close to fun

10 weeks, 15 weeks and 20 weeks sonography

Each of them was stressful as I wondered

How everything inside would be

Nonetheless, as each day passed

We prayed more and gathered more strength

Till one day we were told

That you're viable till the end.

Viable- is that a term to use

For something as precious as you

Who was to enter our lives

And bring in a side to us we never knew.

Nonetheless we waited for our time

to have you with us to hold

And heaven knows it we never forgot

God's kindness and His ways untold

So that was the beginning of Aashna

Our devotion and our true friend

A blessing from above

A thanksgiving which never ends.

Aashna

As we saw you and held you

We understood

How much we loved you

We didn't know we could

Even before you came into being

We knew now what we were not seeing

You completed us

You defined us

You gave us purpose

You gave us tomorrows

And dispelled gloom

And many sorrows

You were sublime

You were supreme

Paramount in our lives

The reigning queen.

Early Years

She had a mind of her own

Is something I came to know

She was never very easy to please

She could break your heart piece by piece

Patience was not her virtue

She would simply decide what she needed to do

Terrible twos came early

And stayed on till rather late

Bringing her up was a roller coaster

And there was a lot on my plate.

The Flip Side of

Her Early Years

An entertainer

A performer

A charmer

A drama queen

A histrionic expert

A friend's friend

She was always full of beans

And her antics would probably

Never end

Her naughty ways

And endless craze

Ensured that there was

Never a dull moment

The clock was always ticking

The wheels of time were turning

And we were just playing our parts

We were growing with her from the start

And soaking in this journey

Of wonder and joy

Fun and frolic

And many a times -panic

Of bringing up this powerhouse of energy

And achieve some synergy

With our friend- Our Aashna!

2021

So the years have flown by

And lo and behold

We have a sixteen -year- old!

An Aashna who brings us

Laughter and joy untold

She has a special charm

And a spark which makes us smile

It is always a pleasure

To walk that extra mile

With every year she passes

She makes us love her more

We've had our fair share

Of arguments and disagreements

There is never a day that goes by

When brick bats do not fly

I guess we are steering her through

The difficult years of adolescence

Where everything the parents say

Just doesn't seem to make sense....

Yet the scale always tilts the balance

Towards love, light and effervescence

The spark and spunk and grit and wit

Everything about her which thrills to bits

As we look at her, we smile and we cry

She will always remain the apple of our eye

Transcending this threshold

From adolescence to adulthood

We wish her wisdom of choice and abundance

And cogent substance and confidence!

SECTION 1

Friends, Foes and Frolic

That One Thread

INSIGHT

Originally written for an aunt's birthday, this poem interweaves my emotions when I saw her idiosyncratic personality. You know that one person who steals the show, highlights the party, secludes all the negativity with light. She was that. She was the fabric that stands out, fearlessly. Something that inspired a thirteen-year-old Aashna in 2017 and forevermore…

There's always that one thread that holds the fabric together,

It stays unmalleable even when the fabric starts to weather,

It is formed in a peculiar way,

It is different, despite the fabric being the same;

There's always that one thread that conveys the message without a scream or shout,

It holds the fabric together,

It is not afraid to stand out

1

Stay And Stay

INSIGHT

This poem is for every partner that loathes their other half leaving. This poem is for every husband that waits, every wife that waits, every child that waits, every friend that stays behind, every lover that cries, every enemy that fights. For they all are as important as us in our own lives, for our lives aren't what they are without them. Without them I lack verbosity, I lack substance, for they make me substantive. They build me up and break me down; both of what I need. They make me me by being them. And them leaving would mean me leaving myself; for they have a part of me and always will. Here is a poem for every person who has made a lifelong memory with another; please don't leave. Ever.

Just stay, will you?

Stay and don't make me blue,

Stay and make golden memories,

Stay and linger a little longer with me,

Grow with me like lichen on wood,

A symbiotic relationship possess we would,

Stay with me like sugar in tea,

Stay as slow as the morning breeze,

Stay with me like the wax of a candle,

Just don't drip, for I may not handle,

Stay with me and be colossal bold,

Stay with me and be silver, be gold,

Stay with me through cultivation and harvest,

Stay with me and give me your best,

Just stay and stay

Just stay and grow,

Just stay,

Don't go.

Adulting

INSIGHT

I went to a school, the same school for seven years. I kept moving in and out and around the country, but always came back to this school. This school always took me. It was my home. During the last two years of my education, I changed schools. It was time to move on – for the better or worse – God will know.

This poem was written as I vibed to sad Hindi songs and stared at a picture of the people – the students, the family I had been with for these years. This poem brought out the best in me. This poem is raw emotion. It is every memory every student hangs on to. It is every bunked class, uneaten tiffin, it is every "stand outside the class" moment, it is every activity, it is every cheer of the sea of people in the auditorium which makes one perform better; this poem is the school. It is the teachers that will stay within me for good and bad; it is every best friend I made and all the gossip that helped no one… but we were all in on it. This poem is an ode to school and school life; it is the transition from a phase where we long to grow up to a phase when we hate adult life. This poem is an ode to adulting.

Ever fear to grow up,

Grow and forget,

Forget to forgive,

Forget to selflessly love,

To stand outside the Principal's office,

To eat in class,

To sleep in class,

Fear of re learning how to love,

Fear of losing touch,

Fear of getting lost in this ocean of life,

Forget the real drops,

Forget the gold memories,

The field trips,

The drama 'practices',

The teacher trouble,

The medals,

The teams,

The games,

The school,

The memories,

Ever fear adulting?

Memories

INSIGHT

This poem is written impulsively, yet accurately, about life and the memories it brings... Of the years passed by and what they meant and the gifts they brought... Of young days and older ones too. The poem originated I was looking at a picture of my 'gang' of friends as a ten-year-old in Kazakhstan — Friends I'll remember and memories I'll cherish; moments that have taken shelter within me.

For times that were sterling and times that were startling,

Cherubic years,

Unnecessary tears,

Cultivated years,

Unwanted fears,

Judgements,

Crucial moments,

Vents and rants,

Vibes and chants,

Travel and stay,

New friends and hunting prey,

Don't worry, newness is key,

For life is still a languid emerald sea.

Letting Go

INSIGHT

A short piece not inspired by anyone but myself. Usually, a cynic to real life emotions and expression of emotions to others, this poem was a revelation. I usually never feel the need to express my feelings and like to keep it that way. But life doesn't work like that. Trust doesn't come naturally to me; and thus, I keep my trouble and worry to myself; but sometimes you just need to let go. You need to share. And no, don't aimlessly keep sharing; share with those who you think truly care and have the best in mind for you. Through this poem I admit I'm a cynic and usually not softened by emotional appeal. But through this poem I also express as much as I can. For, maybe one day, I'll look at the poem as my first step into opening up emotionally.

I fear to indulge, for I've learnt things go,

I fear to indulge for you may not last to and fro,

Expression is nothing but oblivion,

For they've taught me, coldness brings equilibrium,

For your love seems neurotic to me,

For I haven't seen it before, you see,

So bear with me and indulge in every new step of mine,

For maybe I can be the sun and you the sunshine.

2:28:38

- A Group Call

The timing of the call says it all,

Of friendship and love and fun and frolic,

Of late hours, dark rooms, hushed voices,

Of an equilibrium of good and bad choices,

Of sneaks and rides,

Of Low and High tides,

The timing of the call hangs me over with thoughts,

Will we ever call like this again?

Knowing this call will give us no gain,

Ten years hence, Will I remember you?

The friend who knew my fifteen-year-old blues,

Where will you be?

Will I even be?

Will our dreams change like our moods do?

Will I remember you?

Honey Crimson Eyes

I see you,

And your honey crimson eyes,

It's atypical to see a world in two brown spheres,

But maybe, it's because you're my life's biggest sphere,

Sweet like honey

Cutting like crimson,

You're a living oxymoron;

Do they all see it?

Or is it just me?

I see a world in your eyes,

Oceans

Emotions,

Oh wait, what's that?

I see you see me?

Questions Of A Lover

What if one day our emotions aren't enough?

What if we actually put opinions above?

Will you or will you not accept defeat?

Will you accept that your promises of worldly affairs were deceit?

Will you still say you love me the most and forever?

When you know that of love society isn't a firm believer,

Will you still hold me close and fear letting go?

Or is this just the end of our little show?

Is this just irony or should I have expected this?

For mom always said: little boys are little and only there till all is bliss.

Vitamin C

As I sat and chewed on my bitter vitamin C,

It seemed tasteless to me,

Everyday it's sweet then sour,

Like life; every lesson and every hour,

But today was peculiar, for the bitterness faded,

Maybe because I was thinking of a part of me you jaded,

Your bitter words cut down on the taste,

I reprimand you, but my opinions just waste,

The vitamin C was sweeter than you,

Every coin is double sided, it's true,

You knew your bitterness could help me chew.

Why I'd Share
Ice Cream With You

INSIGHT

Going way outside my comfort zone and forte, I've tried to emancipate what goes on in a lover's mind. How a partner, a loved one, looks for you, and thinks about you in every small thing. How a partner sees you in every small thing. Even a thing as small as ice cream. So, here's a quick read on why a person would share ice cream with a loved one.

For you were the one who cried when I cried,

For you were the cloud to my jetty skies,

For you were the one to go pale in my blues,

To love me in all my hues,

You were crimson when I was red and sweet when I was sour,

You knew, loved me in my golden hour, in my darkest hour,

For you sang when I danced and interpreted every glance,

For you were scared to lose me,

That's why, it's not soon that I'm setting you free.

My Person

2:37 am on an early August day,

I hear a song and my mood hits a new high,

As the beats drop and talk of the depth of the scanty streets of the heart;

I search for my streets,

Streets of the heart,

And somewhere in between the parallel streets

That should've never crossed,

There comes a bridge that oversees the trouble and conjoins my path to yours;

Upon my realization dawns the fact that I was on the wrong path all along,

This was my path,

With you and I,

The everlasting sky,

The everlasting bond,

And no goodbye,

So die with me friend, die,

For I can't walk this path alone, it's ours

For this path isn't mine if it isn't yours.

Distance Awakens

INSIGHT

Originally written a singular emotion I thought was felt solely by me, this piece particularly pens the feeling of missing. A feeling, cynics would barely understand. All of sixteen years of age, I decided to recognize myself as a cynic; or perhaps identify as a person who is not exactly emotional; thinking, that emotions are for the weak; and thinking I wasn't that weak.

Little could I decipher, that emotions are what help you overcome. The right emotions can only bring strength. This piece was spurred by my realization that emotion did, in fact, reside within me. It is a piece about missing a friend. A friend gone to a faraway state. The army does make us strong enough to face separation and lose friends; but with some, it's hard, very hard, to let go – just as hard as it is to let go of old habits. You don't realize someone is going until they're gone.

This was my realization.

So this is the part where my conceited self explains emotions and acknowledges you,

There's this tumbling sphere of mellow in my stomach,
usually cynical to softness,

But I guess it's the distance that softens me,

Or maybe knowing you won't be here at my beck and call,

Or maybe it's me morphing into a new phase of life,

Or finally letting you know that your pulchritude has a solid background of your ingrained charm,

Or maybe this is me evolving and learning how to feel, for you only feel when you lack,

Your sojourn into a distant land, away from me has left me emptier than I thought,

In other words, there's this knot in me that ignites once or twice an hour,

In other, cliched words, I miss you.

A First

There's more to life than just you and I,

But tears and swollen eyes complement goodbyes,

I know I bid farewell before satiating the thirst,

But isn't that what makes a first a first?

Hearts were Broken, memories cherished,

Pictures deleted and all thought perished,

And I write this as I set two teens up,

And realize I won't be able to call you while I wait,

Now it's a long-gone bait,

I have regrets; the biggest one being of letting go,

But I'm learning, steady, steadfast and slow,

So bear with me, unforgotten lover; you'll never be a regret,

You're a first I won't forget,

I know I let go too soon, without waiting for thoughts to rush and emotions burst,

But that's what makes a first a first,

So here's to immaturity and my first array of impulsivity.

Color Me You

Not talking off the wall,

Not talking of greatness and worldly possessions,

For I'm no philosopher and know not much of life,

But if it is life that's the case in point,

I do have a few pointers to point,

There'll always be that one person in life,

It won't be a relative, won't be your wife,

It'll be a mate, an acquaintance,

A man to be like you'd want to practice,

It'll be a man under whose influence you'll stutter,

The one who has the power to color you him,

A friend with whom you become them and you don't mind,

They're what you want to be like, illustrious and kind,

No, they aren't your inspiration,

They're your pal, but more than just a pal,

They hold a power over you,

They influence you,

With them you're different,

You're like them,

Becoming more and more like them each day,

A sort of goodness hovers over you,

Their austerity and compassion get to you,

Their persona flies like flu,

It's who they bring out from you,

It's the best of you that they bring out.

Friendship And Doubtful Continuity

Lights thump, the beat drops,

Hearts pumped; we're fresh, new green crops,

The lights changing colours, red, green, blue; a classic disc

fluttering of lights,

Hand in hand, shoulder on shoulder, body on body; all

smiles, all cackles,

The sweat and the bet to dance on and on,

The dance of life, just with heels on,

The music slows down, people tire away, but the ones that

have to stay, they stayed,

Hand in hand, shoulder on shoulder; all smiles; butterflies,

It's our group song, it's our time to shine,

The eternity of youth on my face; youthful sunshine,

In the middle of the sweaty circle, the music slows, my

thoughts come back, a sixth sense rises; a classic disc

emotion,

Glimmering skirts and ties on foreheads,

Drinks in hands, heads in pillowy beds,

I look around, all familiar faces, are they the ones that'll

stand by all my phases?

Is the friendship as strong as my sixth sense prevailed, or as

fragile as the glass that someone just dropped?

But the music, unbothered, never stopped,

So like the musician I didn't either,

This friendship may wither, but for now it's the music, it

doesn't stop, unbothered,

It goes on even when the beat drops,

We're fresh green crops,

Youthful sunshine, butterflies,

As of now, no goodbyes,

No, this friendship may not last forever,

But will forever last forever; a classic disc question

So I make now my forever, come whatever, I don't stop,

So I look around, familiar faces,

I'll miss them when they're gone, or I'll not;

As of now, they're here, familiar faces,

Here to stay or here to go, I really don't know,

Just here to be a part of me, a part of the song, that never

stops, the song of life; a classic disc song,

Youthful sunshine, butterflies but as of now, no goodbyes,

So I dance and I dance, I don't stop,

The moment doesn't stop,

The friendship morphs into a song,

Our song.

SECTION 2

Foresight

Minuscule Voice

INSIGHT

A poem that talks of society and its atrocities, in the subtlest manner, Minuscule Voice is about the little inkling in each one of us which bows to public opinion, to what others will think and its frivolous consequences. It is about society and its seasons of judgments; how fast they change, how little they matter and how regularly they come, just like winter, summer and fall. In the end, even the affected and those shattered by society have to reconcile and get up. They have to refresh and reload. They have to start anew.

Hush, can you hear?

That little voice of sorrow and fear,

It hides behind the mask you wear,

You wear it so society you can bear,

But whatever be, the little voice follows you,

Haunts you, creeps over you, makes you blue,

You've ignored it enough,

Stop now,

Wait,

Watch,

Recover,

Renew,

You, be you.

Nayatara ~

A New Hope Sparkles

INSIGHT

A poem about hope – a cliched topic it is, but the world is deficient of it. This poem glorifies the power of hope. It elucidates the difference of staying in the dark in havoc or staying in it in calm, waiting for the window to break open and sunlight to enter. It's all about the wait. But then again, the wait is the toughest part, isn't it? It's all about the journey and the hope you have, to reach the top. It's all about how you respond in times of hate and grief, not what caused it. In life there are a million things that cause a negative action, but what matters is the positive reaction.

When despotic and when in hate,

A little feeling is shone innate,

When grim with yesteryears' grief,

and when touch seems Christian and brief,

A spark lies tickling your breath underneath,

33

When filled with ugly fear and fuelled anaerobic,

A ray still lies in you, flickering, that you're cherubic,

Nayatara it is… a new star within you,

So when the world is caved up and you knock on its door,

When the sky has lost its hue and you are nothing but blue,

Nayatara is within you… a new star of new origin and new home to you.

The Time Has Come

INSIGHT

This poem reflects a fourteen-year-old Aashna's short sojourn into an environmental revolution. It emphasises how the earth isn't only mine or yours to save; it is OUR world and must be put into order again by US.

It's time we wake up,

We must rise and buck up,

The world awaits our journey, the world awaits our fight,

Let's make just laws, let's make the world abide,

It's not my Earth only, it's your land too,

Let's make the sun shine brighter and the sky a little more blue.

The Shattered Glass, The Shattered Leaf

INSIGHT

A mix of sympathy and sadistic pleasure, this poem is inspired by qualities possessed by humans. It sheds light upon how, when we see a person in misery, instead of helping them out, we shower them with fake sympathy. We have nothing but apathy towards their situation and yet act fraudulently sweet. This does not help. This cages them into their sorrow, and us into our bubble of blindness. Stop this ignorance at once; it's sad if we get pleasure from others' grief and if we do, we're spiteful.

The shattered glass is broken, not repaired yet,

The pieces small, but cut like wounds, not repaired yet,

The glass ain't crying, the leaves ain't pale, they're not morose I bet,

But they're in a bubble of pity and deplorably, now they're morose I bet,

We caged them in a cube of sympathy, they could break free if we weren't there,

They could have been merry, they could have been jovial if we weren't there,

But for whom do we care? Who knows the intention behind our care?

For ribs are broken even with a hug of a bear,

For ribs have been broken even with a hug of a bear.

Castigation And Togetherness

INSIGHT

This poem is an extract of what I wrote for the UN magazine of 2020-21 regarding the start of the Covid-19 outbreak in India, at the time of the Tablighi Jamaat incident. The poem talks of crime and hate speech; and how, social media, instigate people and permeate falsity, which rouses opinions and emotions. This is where we need to stop and look at each situation objectively, without the influence of social media. This also highlights how, in the case of the spread of the Corona Virus in India, communities and people were blamed; how sacrosanct religion is in India and how it takes over; how sacrosanct the media have become to us and how blindly we believe... a case where hate turns amber into a forest fire.

No one spat and no one threw,

Half information doesn't steer but only brews,

A message, a messenger, a video, a creator, a teen, a tween,

Eyes patched on hate; you never know who is behind that screen,

Interweaving religion with social media; adding fury to the fire,

Jumping on the band wagon, is perpetuating desire;

Desire to hurt,

False to blurt,

These voices on the media are bound to nonplus the benighted,

Information has been false and sources not sighted,

Seeing is believing and belief isn't the truth,

Influencing and depriving won't gain you any fruit,

A hospital woman raped,

A doctor blamed,

A new infection claimed,

A community shamed,

The fact that community, religion and diseases we bind,

Proves that to a small room our unity is confined,

'Tis not the time to castigate,

From this situation one must emancipate,

For many will blame and many will play,

But to petty games, we won't fall prey,

We're all in this together after all,

Media and mentality won't make us fall,

For trust is divine and togetherness is key,

Wars can't be waged, for bullets can't set us free.

~A Concerned Global Citizen

Weather

INSIGHT

Taking inspiration from Shashi Tharoor's oratory skills and of course, as the name suggests, the weather. It's funny to me how mood swings lay in small and big things. The weather is one. As the rain falls, tears of happiness and sadness do too. The sun comes out, hope does too. The clouds surge over us and intimidate us. This poem is dedicated to every breeze that blows into my mind and heart and changes my opinions and feelings. It's a poem meant for every rain in which we as children danced, every sunrise that brings about a new day, a new start. This poem is meant to give a 'Filmfare Lifetime Achievement Award' to Weather; it missed out on it.

This weather solicits elation not deprivation,

Morphing between fatigue and apathy, I am indifferent,

The soul oscillates, thinking of hours ahead,

The mind reveres people and places,

All of which it can only possess anon,

The weather demands plaudits not pristine responses,

The dew, celestial and sublime,

Demands to be felt, demands to be smelt,

forthwith; even the outside seems confined,

Nature demands our malicious hands,

Set us free.

Legends Passed On

INSIGHT

Poe, Shakespeare, Tolstoy, grandmothers, TV shows; everything has a story. Every country has a history, every household has a tale, every person shares an anecdote which can't be forgotten. This poem in its truest form is about every story that lingered around me growing up. About tales of the bravery of Guru Nanak Dev ji or of Rudolph the Red Nosed Reindeer. This poem is in short; a summary of the morals and lessons we learnt, and how we remember them.

We learnt not long ago from tales of Dickens,

Those tales were short, taught lessons galore,

In class, maybe, but in life we can't ignore,

For Hamlet and Poe taught us something we know,

For Juliet and Romeo are like arrow and bow,

These legends taught us something,

Sometime back,

Sometime back it was hard to crack,

But now we know, they'll help us in timeless hacks,

For unlike people, places,

Moods and phases,

These stories have our back.

Where Have We Come Now?
~The Cycle Of Life

INSIGHT

This poem, as the name suggests is based on the cycle of life. It depicts how our world revolves around us, but if we look at the bigger picture, we barely constitute anything of the world. Our world is minuscule, our problems, mere minor affairs, our love is nothing, our life is bare compared to the whole world. It asks you an eminent question, that as writers, we write a whole new script; but what about the script of life? Do we write our own, or is our life's script pre destined?

We started as micrometres of liquid,

Lo; forth we were born,

Entered the crawl days,

To the first tantrum and scorn,

Thrown into the swimming pool of life,

45

Sometimes we lived and other times we survived,

The pool turned to an ocean,

And faster was our motion,

Every stroke became a pain,

Not prepared for loss and disdain

To roll in the grass,

Giving family dinners a pass,

To friends who became family,

And songs that became stories,

From being as natural as grass,

To being ostensible,

To writing paragraphs,

Forgetting our first scribble,

We grew up, somewhere between then and now,

Some runners finished the marathon,

Others took a graceful bow,

Memories and memoirs bring transgressions and
contentment,

We grew up somewhere when pain became entertainment,

Where have we come now?

Are we in the midst of a movie, or are we at the climax?

Are we the plot, or the summary itself?

Are we the writers, or merely the book on the shelf?

Metamorphosis

INSIGHT

Change. The only thing that is beyond our control. The only thing we can't even blame on stars and the only thing palm readers can't read. This poem merely highlights its inevitability and how drastic or minor it can be; how every differing thought leads to change and how every unheard and heard voice does too. This poem is about the growing of a bud into a flower and mankind into a humanity.

It's funny how small things bring a change

A drastic one

A slight one

A mild one

A bold one

But just a peculiar sort of uncomprehended change

A change you rue

A change you knew

A change that's sweet or one that's bitter

A change emboldens or makes you a quitter

Desires Of A Daffodil

INSIGHT

As I sat on the swing in my garden; looking for inspiration in life and literature, I came across a daffodil; it's fierceness and mildness together in one, caught my eye. Do plants, non-mobile beings, go through more than we do? And even if they do, what is their breaking point? What is their saturation level? What is their burning point, like how we burn? This poem goes out to every daffodil in my life, one that stood like a pillar but was as soft and beautiful.

The daffodil

Planted uphill

Acclimatized to survive the worst

Survives the rain, survives the frost

It shields the grass

Like iron and brass

But brass burns too

The daffodils strength is limited and blue

It can't conquer fear over this fire

For going beyond its yellow color is its sole desire.

Whatever Will Be

Won't Be

INSIGHT

Que Sera Sera was the song of the era my mother grew up in; and through her, it was my childhood song as well. A lullaby I truly didn't understand till very late, it was a rhyme I nonetheless sang mindlessly. And once I did understand it, I wrote about it. This poem is inspired by my understanding of it. Here's to letting life take its own turns without dictating any bit of it; but, knowing the turns and not wandering about. Here's to my motion against the song and all it taught.

The power of now is seldom tomorrow,

So now isn't the time to grieve past sorrow,

Think today and enlighten furthermore,

Fly today and tomorrow you soar,

For life's not a song, but a farfetched sea,

Que sera sera, whatever will be won't be,

For static ain't this sea,

So now is when you live your dream,

Que sera sera lays a myth,

Little girl, grow up; life's a sharp scythe,

You're the grass it cuts;

So please no ifs and buts,

Que sera sera, whatever will be won't be,

Think of the future,

Darling, it's yours to conquer and see.

Some Clouds, Some Trees

INSIGHT

A poem written in protective and hopeful emotion, this short yet meaningful piece is an essential read. It's a poem which talks of how doubt is important but it must never get the better of us. It tells the reader, that your blunders can't be ignored – no, they can't; in life you must not fall into the trap of false hope. Yet it highlights that there will always be trees larger than your mistakes to give shade to you. The shade of correction. The trees here are the people and things that protect us in life. The real ones.

Some clouds are good and some are bad

When bad clouds come don't be grim and sad

For there'll be trees that save you from the thunder

Those trees are bigger, taller than your blunders

These trees that shade you from clouds are love

They're more imperative than the clouds above

Prodigious Awareness

They tell you you've matured,

They tell you you've lost weight,

They tell you you've listened to the angel on the shoulder,

But do they tell you what waits ahead is a boulder,

That you've gained weight not lost,

That you've become darker, that your actions will cost,

For people are good when they want to be,

To not enlighten you of your mistakes,

Is worse than praises and high held stakes,

Shake up,

Wake up.

Judgements And How They Kill

Every eye has a peculiar story,

One you probably are unaware of,

Yet you muster up its gore,

Do you realize the sting of your prerequisites?

You called me something I wasn't, will never be,

You told tales of my days, whose insights you'll never see,

My past and future determined, inferred by you,

For tall tales and great legends, making me seem blue,

Your judgments are killing and it's time you know,

For feelings are unfeigned not for show,

A strong wall I was, or so I believed,

Until you hit me with mild bullets, left me bereaved,

People got nothing on me, or so I thought;

Who knew my life, by your judgment could be bought?

A Thread Of
My Knitted Star

My star is me

Made of thread tightly knitted

A thread of culture

A thread of literature

A thread for life

A thread for glim

Each vivid, none grim

But forth shines a sword, not one like the rest

Lo' a thread dangled out

It wasn't the same

It maybe the thread of life or death or one I'm still to tame

It stood conspicuous

Not stiff just different

Maybe not one I'd thought would filter forefront

But here it is... yet a part of me

A little foreign

A little bleak

But with time it'll gain color and maybe life too

For the star still stands out despite the sky being blue.

SECTION 3

Feminism, Freedom And Social Flaws

I Am

INSIGHT

A woman has the power to say much with few words. She isn't obliged to possess verbosity; her word leads to a thousand ideas. This poem authentically describes the aspirations, raging agony, happiness, loneliness in a full room and most of all, the pride of a woman. Written by a fifteen-year-old me for the UN young women column of my school, as I wrote I didn't look back, didn't re read for each word in this poem is a string of my heart. You pull it, the heart dismantles. This poem is one of my favourites and despite women empowerment being a cliched topic, this poem possesses the power to move many young girls, or so I hope.

I am who I am

No matter what they say

I am who I am

For a boy child you may pray.

As a child I thought I was free, free of all inhibitions;

But little did I know that a boy was, supposedly,

God's greatest creation;

I was free, I was born free, I am free; give me my liberation!

Walking down to school, he was stronger than me;

Seeing the 'strong boy' the world was in glee

I was smarter, better, Brighter than him,

But at that, there wasn't glee, it all seemed dim.

Yes, a woman marries a man

But a man marries her too

 So why does she raise the child alone,

The child's shades include his hues.

And for a week every month, she's considered impure;

But for a man's eminent issues, there's always a cure;

She fights her battles day after day, with nothing but a smile as shield

So why is manual work still considered a man's field?

I am a woman, simple and pure;

And this time my shield are my fellow victims for sure;

I am who I am and I have no regret,

I am who I am and this injustice I shall not forget.

Today we rise, together, forevermore

Today we fight and tomorrow we grow.

An Ode To No

INSIGHT

We have all heard the phrase 'no means no'; but just like the Indian government, we don't implement it. This poem is more of a 'thinking out loud piece', in which I am trying to explain to myself and others, how you don't need to say yes to anything out of nicety or politeness. Sometimes it is wiser to be the bad one but refuse something you don't accept or want. This poem not only reflects on small things like a pencil or food but the bigger things in life. This poem is trying to portray how Indian society revolves around accepting what we don't need, how we are obliged to say yes to anything and everything – from marital rape to the forceful Aunty's pakora.

If you can't, you won't, so just say NO

Saying a no is much easier than you know

You may feel guilty, you might feel mean

It's better than feeling listless and not saying what you mean

It's not a long hard word, just a simple NO

But if you still can't stop the snow, well then, as they say, let it snow.

Life In A Locker Room

INSIGHT

A few adolescent boys and girls; shattered the hopes to a hopeful youth and scared parents furthermore, more than they already are of social media and teenage. A few pictures, a few words, a tinge of hatred shook up India and made it realize the power of social media. This poem is an expression of fear, the fear a thousand other girls shared with me. The fear of being prey to these vultures who have no control over themselves and I have no damage control.

I've seen it on news, I've seen it on the net,

My heart still silenced and my mind nothing but a mess,

Is this what locker room talk is? Is this even normal talk after all?

If twisting a post into a tale is a trend, then I'm going to have a fall,

If I thought before I sent every picture to anyone I knew,

It would steal my nature away from me, it would steal me away from me,

I don't want life to be a memory of me simply remembering days of glee,

I want to live happily,

Worry free,

In presence of men and women alike,

In presence of elation and deprivation to fight,

I want to be able to send whatever I want,

All I need is help to rectify,

To differentiate between the good and the bad girls and boys,

But how can I when even good girls support the bad boys?

When my own aren't with me,

I do not expect any glee,

I come from a family, supportive and encouraging;

The fact that they were concerned, was in itself enraging,

First I questioned and then pondered myself,

I too would be scared for my child's health,

And no not the health that makes us look like models,

But mentally, to be alright or not; sentimental or strong,

This incident though didn't occur around me has scarred me and shaped my thoughts,

Has made me question the morality of my mates,

All the forthcoming play dates,

All the people in the bubbles of the net,

All the people who may just be a threat,

It shouldn't be this way but can we actually help it?

Yesterday it was a chat, tomorrow it may be an experiment,

Yesterday it was talk, today it may be action,

Please don't make me lose in humanity, all my compassion.

The Change

INSIGHT

As an Indian girl, this poem is for every Indian girl and boy. It's the fear I feel when I step out... It's the anxiety we get as a society due to rape and sexual injustice... It's how helpless I feel; how shameless I feel; thus, the only courage I muster up is to spit out words like such. These words can't change the conditions of the harmed survivors; but maybe, just maybe, it can save another woman from harm and another man from crime. This poem is about how the bloom in a lady is crippled... How she lives despite no life... How she cannot flourish anymore; and more so about how close to nothing is done by those who can actually do something.

As on November 2020:

32,500 cases of rape
Indian courts disposed of only about 18,300
127,800 cases pending

The change we talk of,

The hope we renew,

Is nothing but a myth...

For rapists may not, but change favours the bold,

The blood just trickled down the first time,

You aren't too old,

Yet the vulture bites off your organs with thoughts
unconsidered,

Unconscious,

Unassisted,

Unaware;

The marks he left are crude and bitter,

What's left is the memory; a nightmare to be sought,

Who knew the blooming, budding flower would crumble,

Who thought?

Male // Unmale

INSIGHT

Originally written on demand and further published in TIS Magazine, this poem is every modern Indian person's guide to moralistic living. It talks of how stereotypes exist for men as well. How a 'conventional', 'normal' man should behave. As we speak of unleashing women from stereotypes and traps, we must acknowledge the same for men. This poem isn't meant to sensitize, it's simply stating the obvious, it's telling you what you should already know in the 21st century. Every man is different. They too can cry and it won't project them as weak. There's so much more to it than just tears.

If I can cry, so can he,

No rule written against it, not even with thee,

Adhering to fear is not female,

For pain and sadness, there's no measuring scale,

A man sheds tears; oh how female;

Masculinity apart, fears to depart,

There aren't traits confined to gender and more,

A man's no less a man if he's crumbled and sore,

For masculinity apart, this thought is toxic and grim,

A man's no less a man, when a woman's strong and he dim,

Violence and hate aren't traits to be sought,

'Tis the time of the youth,

This process of thought can't be bought.

Alive And Dying ~

A Poem on Society

My confidence takes shelter under my clothes

My happiness recedes, remains in my home

When I walk out the door of my abode

I feel throttled as I breathe

I choke underneath

I despise the touch of any beholder

I despise an eye beholding upon me

I am afraid; to say the least

Afraid of the rebel scattered within you

Afraid of the scattered pieces coming together

To come and scatter me again, again

For poets write and anchors confront

But only a victim knows beyond the forefront

Periods should make me bleed

Not men

I am a woman, not a rat in a tiger's den

And if life is a den after all

I'm not the rat

Come witness that.

Who Are They?

Hush little girl,

She shouldn't make your eyes red and sore,

You know it isn't veracity, you are much more,

Why do you cry despite solace?

Oh no don't howl,

It isn't your fault her dirty mouth is foul,

You're worried she meant what she said?

Is that the reason you're sad to bed?

Well, I bet it's not that, she didn't mean to be mean,

Darling, everyone isn't you; the world is mean,

Their scrutiny and faux pas don't matter,

Remember, we despise the latter,

And if despite that you cry,

Then they've succeeded in breaking you;

Oh you wouldn't give in, would you?

And every night if you cry and then you pray,

Think and think again,

Who even are they?

To The Lady In Red

Honey your face talks words unspoken,

Your wrinkles tell me of all the hearts you've broken,

And as you sway to the beat of the drums; subtle yet loud,

You sway and create around you a persona and clout,

People look at you inevitably

Waiting for their hearts to be broken, inexhaustibly,

Contemptible little buffoons they must be,

You create yourself anew each time; beyond you they just can't see,

Inexperienced; they baffle and lose their wit,

Each step of the way, you lessen their grit,

You're on your own, in your own monolith of steel and glass,

But everyone wants to be in your building, it's hard to surpass,

You don't budge,

Yet they indulge,

It's the vibe you sought,

Sorted, confident, like you don't care,

And to burst your bubble, they just don't dare.

Where Do I Stand?

Inspired by the Hathras Rape incident
(14 September, 2020)

In a hierarchy that goes from cows to rape, where do I stand?

In a fabric that goes from caste to quota, where do I blend?

In a country undignified for women, how many trigger warnings should I send?

In a state where a minor and major alike; paralyze, fight, confess, die,

In a state where I can only cry,

My respect decried,

My honour taken,

No man forsaken,

My impurities defined,

My freedom confined,

In a country where flashes are in the wrong direction, where do I stand?

In a country where protests are washed over like fire, where do I stand?

In a country, where rape is chosen to be hidden,

What is allowed and what is forbidden?

SECTION 4

Family – A Warm Familiarity

Dear Indu

INSIGHT

One of my few poems actually dedicated to someone, this poem is for my main homie, the person closest to me – Nani, my grandma. More than the social barrier of relationships and the load they carry, she's a friend, a confidant. Not a conventional 'chill' adult but modern in her own ways and jovial in all ways. Not only did I grow up in front of her but grew with her. She acts my age with me when needed, acts hers when needed. If not the biggest, one of the biggest factors of my wholesome life. Indu.

Dear Indu,

You've been so amicable towards me that I stay indebted forever,

Your smile ever charming adds to your beneficial sort of endeavour,

You playing with your phone like it's a toy to be sought,

Golden memories aren't the only thing from you I have bought,

Your laugh morphs emotions from grim to elated,

Your heart forever big and your gloom leaves me slated,

Dear Indu,

You've held a baby Aashu and you hold my heart captivated still,

So you can keep me forever and more,

We can sail and sail aimlessly; with no shore,

Tugging on your rosary and telling on the beads,

Potting plants in gardens and stopping me from eating seeds,

The red light above your bed,

Making sure Nanu eats his med,

Holding me then and holding me now,

Growing with me again, then and growing with me now,

Dear Indu,

You clear a mist of miasma with a word so sweet,

Teaching a raccoon how to eat, how to greet,

You live and solicit life,

Being a mother, Nani and wife,

Love is all I have to give,

So accept my humble thrift,

For love, I always wish, lasts

Even through your mah-jong games and endless fasts.

1 Fear

INSIGHT

This poem came to me as a rush of emotion rather than regular writing. It's an appreciation towards our parents, our guardians, those who knowingly, unknowingly protect us. It then morphs into doubt and says that the glass wall (parental protection) is reeding thin, it's going away as we adult our way into life.

Trapped in the cage of a promising tomorrow,

Today has been shattered and replaced with sorrow,

We live in a glass box, with a glass ceiling and a glass floor,

But as soon as we start to enjoy the view, there's a knocking on the glass door,

It's from the world outside, not your world within,

They try to conjure for what is right and wrong,

But the glass wall shields you, the glass wall reeding thin,

I fear it will break,

But for heaven's sake,

It protects you for now, it protects you from within,

The glass wall shields you, the glass all reeding thin.

The Mean Mom

INSIGHT

Feelings towards a mother are subjective and change every so often; with every action, a new feeling. This poem is about how mothers have to put up a harsh front to mould you; for the better, for the best. It's about how the mean mom succeeds in building you up, correcting you and making you what you are and will be. The mean mom is the real mom. She stops you from what is wrong and knows that you'll hate her for it then, but thank her later. She's ready to partake the hate and give love in a disguised form instead.

She was mean and harsh and overly involved

Her ideas were fixed and ideals never revolved

She had to know all your friends; no strangers allowed

She knew what you posted and what you said in a crowd,

She forced the piano lesson, down your throat

She said "life is nothing without a sport"

You rolled your eyes as she talked to your mates

She was the meanest mom, just in your fate

But thank your stars she was mean and brutal

Otherwise, life would be sore; personality crucial

Your posture is straight, your mannerisms just fine

So you've got a mean mom and that's the sign

Your friends are normal

Thank God they're formal

You're a good guest and as good a host too

That certainly means, your momma loved you

A mean mom she was and thank God for that

Rules Of Pride

1. When they acknowledge you show no sign of knowledge, don't be pompous, be precautious

2. Every smile you make, every head you shake, leaves an impact; don't come across as a snob, engage the mob

3. When you know you're doing well, you don't act shy neither do you swell

4. Results aren't harbingers of change, the graph of work is; fill your home with not successful fog, but your days of slog

5. Family rejoices upon pay, but let the serfs not celebrate with you; keep them at bay

6. Keep a tactful eye on opponents and rank holders, but disguised with a content front remains the beholder.

As You Grow, As I Go

As his hair dyes change and chest hair grey,

As his teeth weaken but clothes remain stiff,

As his back hunches, but he's insistent on extra crunches,

As he is tender, but seldom agrees to being soft,

As his eyes water when I leave our home; our loft,

As he sees my first baby step video all over again,

Rewatching every second, thinking he has new seconds to gain,

As he holds my first salary's first gift to him,

As he sees me through sorrow and helps me when I'm grim,

As he drops me with a boy and waits till I come home,

Unaware, his hawk eye watch makes me feel more at home,

Then as he realises, he's dropping me for real this time,

No waiting this time, no ice cream when I'm back, no crazy new spying hack,

This time I'm GOING, going for good,

Wedded and suited, away from childhood,

The bride to be I will be,

And he, the father of the bride,

He'll try not to break the coconut for a man's gotta keep his pride,

But as the last song plays,

The last dance slays,

The coconut shell breaks, his tender self, exposed,

It's time for my goodbye,

And this time papa, I know you're going to cry.

SECTION 5

Films

Kabira

It's funny how when people fail, songs bring emotions to you,
Kabira;

A feeling in itself, a surge of nostalgia and forgotten friendships,

Ones we thought will last forever,

Ones we gave up for,

Ones we gave in to,

Ones with our Bunny and Aditi,

Ones we got no return from but still knowingly invested into,

"Kaise teri khudgarsi, na dhoop chune na chao"

Phrases that make your heart pound with an array of thoughts and feels,

Friendships and ambitions;

When friendships become ambitions,

When we still have hope and say, "kabira manja,"

When our hope shatters and we say "kabira yu na ja,"

When Naina's tears aren't sufficient,

When nothing but bolting is efficient,

That is when one realizes,

These aren't friendships after all,

This is a series of bountiful love that has made these friends family,

A friend returned; an emotion swam back into your ocean of emotions.

Sapne

"Ma'am, I want to become an actress"

"Ma'am, I want to become a doctor"

"Engineer"

"I want to be like Bill Gates"

"Ambani"

Big dreams, big words,

When is it that we forget about these words?

When do they become mere words?

When do they 'undream' their way out of our lives,

When does the guitar stop strumming?

When does the pressure elevate in our lives?

When does fresh mist become miasmal?

When does language become abuse?

When do dreams become locked, forgotten rooms?

Open that door,

Let the dream flow,

Unchain yourself,

Thoda rukh ke dekh zara,

Bemalang tera iktara.

Pal

To a day that is gone,

To the day I hated,

To the day I was born,

To the day with juvenescence I greeted,

To a day that's dead,

To a day I lied,

To a day I spent solely in bed,

To a day I cried,

Cried till tears ran out,

To a day I fought,

To a day I till date doubt,

To a day I first bought,

A thought about the magnanimity of life,

To a day I found myself a wifey and a real wife,

To a day I'll remember,

Good, bad, crazy or sad,

A day that made up my life,

A day in which I yearned to thrive,

All of it,

Even the bad bit,

I crave it;

What will happen tomorrow?

Will there be sorrow?

Will it be a mélange of sad songs?

So let's borrow from today, what we are permitted to borrow,

The days,

That's all this piece of emotion says.

Rooh

INSIGHT

The poem is far more than its monotonic name. A poem about life and the uniqueness it seeks, is trying to tell the reader that differences are good. You don't have to be the same as another. You don't have to be like 'them'. Unleash your superman, rise and flourish in your own skin, doing your own thing.

The soul often solicits change not ordinary,

There wasn't ever an average, we moulded it,

No love is normal,

No culture is formal,

No passion is common,

No man indifferent,

The soul solicits difference,

My soul likes fire and yours ice,

I rue pain and you suffice,

Our paths don't diverge into a yellow wood,

They never started together, they never would,

Har rooh ke andar ek naya sa parinda hai,

Khol ke dekho, ud ke dekho.

Small Things Break My Heart

INSIGHT

Mid-March

Setting: swinging on my favourite swing in the garden; mid-March 2020;
Lockdown, Covid Times:

As I swung faster and faster on my favourite swing and only resort during the anxious lockdown times, I looked all around me in last hope of inspiration or aspiration. The lockdown for me was more than introspection and goody goody things. It was different. I grew after it. When I think about it now, it was a time of immaturity and amateurism. I'm glad it's gone, but one thing it instilled in me was thought provoking writing and good music taste. I wrote this sad yet articulate piece in midst of the daily dose of nature I could get in my garden in Covid Times. As I heard birds and bees chirp, my heart chirped too; just not in the same mellow and jolly way.

They say heartbreak is huge and supposedly aches,

Well ache it may, but a routine it is,

Every minuscule thing breaks me a little bit,

Every chirping bird, the thought of it going one day,

Every friend and friendship, the thought of its ruin,

Every old man sitting in a boat,

Oblivious to when it will sink,

Every poet, scared of his fading ink,

Every word I say and how it may not matter years hence,

Every sparrow, ocean, sunrise and every decaying possession,

For we too are decaying possessions,

For we too possess happiness and joy,

And we decide either of which we are, today, tomorrow,
forever.

SECTION 6

Fauj

He Didn't Choose Me

~ To the strong families of the departed
Written right after the martyrdom of the Galwan Heroes

He promised me promises, now deceased,

Of my dreams and our dreams, which now are ceased,

Of children and a home, now both shattered,

Of happiness and contentment, now merely scattered,

But I have no shocked vein in me for I knew I never came
first;

He swore to prioritise his nation and her every thirst,

I can't be demanding; my kids, strong yet unfaithful,
unkeen,

Insightful that their father was a man in the olive green.

Selfless Independence

Happy Independence Day Bharat

To the man that served not for him but for us,

To the man with ruptured organs, silent, creating no buzz,

To the child that's fatherless,

A wife who's rudderless,

To an incomplete family for a complete nation,

To sacrifice beyond your imagination,

To the man that buried his independence for you and nothing more,

To every fighter, on land, air and shore.

For you we pray every day, every way,

So here's wishing you a Happy Independence Day.

Dear Kashmir

INSIGHT

It was a casual winter evening for my mom and me as we lived the quintessential SF (separated family) life within the cantt. We went to TOI to watch the latest movie which at that time was 'Uri - The Surgical Strike.' As we drove back, my rage increased and as it did, the only outlet I had was to pen it down. As mom spoke to dad on a faraway border, I wrote an open letter to the highest authority my thirteen-year-old self could think of; the Chief of Army Staff. I wrote to him a poem with the whole backstory and a small unimportant introduction. As I showed it to my mom in hope, with glistening eyes, I got quite the opposite response. "I can't just send it to the Chief and he doesn't have the time to read every thirteen-year-old's patriotic poem Aashna," my mom said. But I was my father's daughter after all; so pushy I was and I did push my way through. Somehow, the Chief took out the time and somehow this poem landed up in the annual AWWA AVNI journal. And ever so grateful I was and still am to him and the team for amplifying the youth's voice by giving a willing representative an eager chance. So, this as I call it, is my 'poem of pride' the first of many to be officially published and read. An ode to Kashmir and the anger it brought in me.

With your fruits and nuts and Chinar leaves

We cherish them and graze the tall deodar trees

111

The northernmost you are, up, up very high

For you and your people our men graze the sky

Our kings become stars for you and only you

But as you would say... That's just past and the story
continues to brew

For you we have fought, with an unbroken will

And all we can hear are voices that are still

Instead of claps, we met with stones

Instead of talk, we've broken bones

Time and again we've proven to you

But yet again our zeal has just flown through

Giving up is still an option; but if we do, YOU suffer

It's not a war for us but it is one we fight for you and what
you offer

We don't benefit much, but yes, you can still sleep sound

Because we are the Indian Army and to be your guardians
we are bound.

Why?

To The Indian Army Serving in Kashmir

Why is it that despite our warmth,

We meet with stones and fight in swarms,

Why do we carry bullets galore,

When none are needed, we've lost the war,

Why are we disguising in Kaftaans,

Yet on the other side are your sultans,

Why do we lose our literal lives,

When you've killed us without knives,

But vigilance for you is key,

For hard to fulfil is your plea,

To kill an immortal is a hard task to do,

For you will always be the dirty imprint of his polished shoe.

21 Years And Forevermore

Kargil Divas

Today we fight for every life taken

And every step blown on the glorious way

Today we might be sober and shaken

But lest we forget work of a soldier, night and day

It's been 21 years

Of courage and tears

Fatherless new-borns and widowed broken fears

The stomp of heavy boots

Guns and farfetched shoots

Clad in Camouflage, aiming at the flag

No fear of when they'll come back

Families awaiting the arrival of a hero

In a body bag or body clad, oblivious this remained

The only sure path was victory proclaimed

And victory we got

Hard we fought

Jai Hind!

Azaad Hindustan

To Every Ill-Influenced Kashmiri Who Doubts India

He said hello from the other side,

To heaven's rules he could not abide,

To live in valleys of heaven was hell for him,

Without war chants, it all seemed dim,

The grass is always greener on the other side,

To heaven's rules, he could not abide,

The crescent moon, outdid the Tricolour,

Authenticity faded, the vision was blurrier,

Sobriety and solace began to hover,

The face of reality threw off its cover,

So he threw a stone at the olive green, thinking what difference would it make?

But that is what a thousand other Kashmiris did for freedom's sake,

For the grass is always greener on the other side,

To heaven's rules he could not abide,

Since then, a question lingers in the air,

आज़ाद हिन्दुस्तान कहाँ है?

Hameen Ast-O

*"Agar firdaus bar roo-e zameen ast,
Hameen ast-o hameen ast-o hameen ast..."*

*If there is a paradise on earth,
It is this, it is this, it is this...*

The man in the shikara, wearing a kaftaan, sings this melody,

As I row in the Dal,

The terror sleeps in the yellow, crimson trees,

The loss possessed by the land morphs into beauty,

The ruins proclaim, the city was once alive,

The people proclaim, they're suffering,

Birds flown away,

Houses left to decay,

But heaven does lay here,

If only hell hadn't taken over,

The devil and angel fight over nature here,

The people become the victims,

The little boy offering tea in a decaying pot,

The man who tells me he was once shot,

Both hot; one on my taste buds, the other with anger,

The anger it is,

The suffering it is,

That is the secret to this rueful aesthetic,

That is Kashmir,

A mixture of heaven and hell,

A mixture of the good and the bad,

If there's a paradise of a sort on earth, it's here

A philosopher in words depicted my view,

Kashmir, o Kashmir,

This one's for you.

SECTION 7

Flights And Voyages:

Musings Related To Travel

The Roads And Its Gifts

INSIGHT

We all have been on road trips. We all have heard the classic Indian package of road trip songs. We all have eaten the classic mom's road trip sandwiches. We have all lay down on the backseat and folded our legs up a window against the blazing sun; with no noise but the music playing. This poem was an idea that occurred to me on the road. Enroute to Chandigarh all I could think of was all the emotions a mere road trip brings about. A single road trip can change mindsets – we've all seen that in movies and songs; but it's reality. A single road trip can bring about a whole new feeling and new, different thoughts and revelations.

The road I travel on solicits a change in me,

Every time, persistently, every time,

Often in a cloud of evocation,

When you're so driven by the past that you forget what lies ahead,

Where your tires roll into memories and only memories,

This cloud I wish wouldn't burst,

This cloud is what we thirst,

But seldom does it become a constant,

For life isn't constant,

The road is changing,

The car is moving,

So should you.

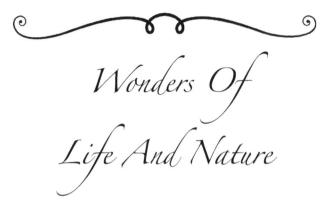

Wonders Of Life And Nature

INSIGHT

Being an army kid, my dad was always posted to distant places. Faraway, in borders and valleys, with danger and daring spirit; nonetheless extremely beautiful. Once, papa was posted in a place called Pooh; just at a little distance from Sangla Valley. We camped at Sangla once for two days. Amidst the pinecones and tents and bonfire all one could ponder upon was the newness of nature. In Delhi you can hardly see stars let alone count them. This poem was written by an Aashna who was star gazing, wondering when will she ever be able to come back to this dynamic, majestic valley of sparks, stars and nature.

Amidst the rays of a crimson sun,

I see where you are,

Where were you before?

Magnificent tall, with broad leaves,

Each of these mustard leaves sing a melody,

Each line of the melody, portrays a caramel coated story,

A story of pain,

A story of gain,

A story of love,

Of the ones watching us above,

The shepherds pass by and so does the herd of sheep,

Quintessentially they walk, but each head turns, trying to capture a glimpse of you,

Amidst the autumn trees,

I see where you are,

Where were you before?

Peacocked trees surround you, but your sober green stands out,

You blossom in your truest form,

Authentic, alive, alert,

Amidst the pale brown sky,

I see where you are,

Where were you before?

Your leafless body is shone in the morning and shimmered at night,

All men pass by, some with a cumbersome sigh,

But you leave each one baffled,

Your beauty lies unknown,

For when it is known,

Man may hunt you, like he usually does,

Thus you're safe here,

In your truest form.

The Land Of Sugar And Love

- Spiti, Himachal, 2018

'Tis the land of sweetness,

As it says in the name,

With its great mountains comes greatness,

Indifferent beauty from the people to the yak's mane,

The high terrains, the not so broad roads,

Makes one forget; this equilibrium is result of firepower and swords,

The Indus passes by, each bubble sings a song,

Each song; a story of the past and the present,

Tells a passer-by, leave the future, the climb is long,

Naked trees break the moon and make it more crescent,

The sweet smell of apples fills the sugar sector,

The crunch of the almond, the softness of the pear,

The people make you warm, the cold no more a factor,

This place has mesmerising magic; this understatement isn't fair!

Around And Around

My dreams aren't bottled and never will be,

I want to travel mountain to sea,

I want to fly every airline,

Sydney to Vancouver,

Life's got no cover,

I'll see the tallest tip and the deepest point, alone or maybe with you,

We can jump off docks in Maine,

Or play pretend in Spain,

With Spanish girls around you

And yes, me too,

Let's go somewhere we can pretend, where ostensibly we can play,

Where we aren't just pots that lay and decay,

Let's go somewhere we like,

Up a slope, on a hike,

Let's go see snow in Astana,

And be morose in Kabul,

But when in Rome, do as the Romans say,

And when in Istanbul, you pray and pray,

Location to location,

Can life be an endless vacation?

Around and around let's go,

Chile to Soho,

With you,

With me,

Oceans and seas,

Birds and bees,

Forests and Lanes,

Mother Russia in Ukraine,

Gnocchi in Sicily,

Pizza in Chicago,

People in Prague,

Wine in Italy,

Key characters being you and me,

All that matters is you and me.

Leaving A Piece Of Me

Every place I move,

Every new journey I take,

Every new cantt I move to,

Every new friend I make,

Every public school I join,

Consumes a piece of me;

It's this sojourn into reality on sunny days,

That I look back and reminisce upon the piece I left,

The piece ignites once or twice, when I tend to miss,

I miss the most when the past reaches such eminence that missing becomes a habit,

I miss the different weathers,

The variety of sunlight,

The people,

It all has a piece of me.

Four Beers Down

Four beers down and my emotions turn real,

Every step taken isn't shaky but has feel,

Gobbled up sorrows out in a river down my cheeks,

Four beers down, life isn't as smooth and sleek,

What I felt I always knew,

But four beers down what I felt I realize,

The future is actualized,

Future of the decisions taken now, visualized,

Thus the tears,

Thus the fears,

Thus the real me,

Four beers down, enrages the sense of feeling free.

SECTION 8

Focus –
Before And After The Pandemic

Inspiration

I wander around,

I wander about,

A nameless TinTin with no map and no Snowy,

Just grey faced beasts around me and thoughts ought to be flowy,

In the dullness of oblivion I find color,

I find big exultations even in a tiny cruller,

Strangers I see, in cafes around me,

New air I breathe, New pollution, New sea,

Morphing into deep thought as I observe,

Each oscillation of a new tree,

Each his own person, nothing but free,

That's a pro of a new land,

No one knows you, you don't know a strand,

So as I feed on the cruller,

So as I see every shade and every new color,

People replace treats and become food for thought,

That's where poetry beams and I become paisley,

That's when inspiration finds new personality.

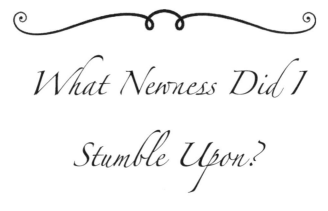

What Newness Did I

Stumble Upon?

*A Short Account On Understanding Others
And How It Changed Me*

Vulnerability doesn't morph like emotions,

It's introduced into us, as and when we lack,

Until yesterday I was certain I wasn't the type to shed tears and sweat over people,

Until yesterday I was sternly handling loss and gain,

I was sure small changes could cause no pain,

Until yesterday I looked down upon mates crying over other mates,

Until yesterday I quailed at dressing up for silly dates,

Until yesterday I laughed at a friend cry over a man,

I'd be baffled as to how much she adores him and doubted how she can;

Then I grew, understood much more, understood reasons,

Moods and change of seasons,

Understood attachment and relations,

Witnessed mismatched equations,

And luckily wasn't prey to this sort of a game,

And for that myself, I'd gladly blame,

So now, I'm less surprised as I console the same friend over the same person yet again,

For through age I succumb, I have more wisdom to gain,

But of what I reap from being a third person in these cases, is empathy and so I talk in past tense,

I gained wisdom early and I write hence.

I Pack Again –
After A Year, For School!

I packed,

Yes I packed,

But for posterity this time,

Packed in the yellow emblemed books with the now sordid scribbles, earlier called handwriting,

Packed in the translucent pouch which earned Rastogi another buck when pre boards and I were fighting,

Packed in the bright blue lunch box, casually called tiffin,

Packed in my sorrow post converging, this time the authority wasn't bluffin',

Packed in a ton of memoirs,

And a dozen old au revoirs,

Packed in hope, earlier bottled in a WHO bottled liquid,

Packed in the glistening future, which doesn't seem as wicked,

My bag's heavy now, with a bottle, a lunchbox and muck filled notebooks,

With the colloquial project I came up with a night prior,

With the gruesome pain of the year gone by, causing nothing but tire,

So I pack my bag and wear the grey and blue,

Wishing I'll get nothing but the brightest hue.

Wait

And as a beat drops,

As a new face into my life pops,

As a new eye glistens,

As a new bird chirps and I just listen,

I wait;

As a string strums another

And a sting bites and falls another feather,

As a bug crawls on,

And women walk with new shawls on,
I wait;

I wait for my old thoughts to morph into new ones,

I wait;

But the only things changing are people, places and other nouns,

I hate,

I hate The wait,

But inevitably I wait;

I wait for a single message and a single picture,

I give up a lot to wait but the wait only stretches,

Waiting to find new inspiration and thought,

Waiting to blabber away and what not,

Waiting for passion,

Waiting with compassion,

Just waiting away,

Wasting hours away,

An hourglass ticks as I wait to sway,

Sway in metamorphic thought,

Neurotic thought,

Over anything; someone, something, maybe a possession I bought,

But wait gives way to wait and only wait;

So tell me dear reader,

Tell me how much more,

How much more till I soar,

Like the bird I watch and the time ticking away in my watch,

How much more till I write with passion,

How much more of this transgression,

How much more throwing of sheet in aggression,

How much till I learn anew and afresh,

How much can I wait

How long is this bait?

And here my cycle dispatches into another long cycle,

This period is hard to tackle,

So as I listen to a new song, a new lyric, a new beat, a new spree,

My last resort is thinking this is the last time wait hangs over me,

So help me as I succumb wait,

As I wait,

As I wait for the end of this bait.

Ambition

With classes changed and work ways switched,

A lost corner discovered amidst a global illness,

The cure to my preceding problems lost among many lives,

The illness killing people and killing qualities,

The illness causing a new illness, the illness of ill thinking
and lethargy,

Moods swinging like winds and minds as metamorphic and
weatherly,

As the cure is invented, reinvented; rejected; reprimanded; so
is my ambition,

Just when I think I'm ready to face the screen, just when I
refilled the engine of life,

I ran out of gasoline, it wasn't as clean, all messy and fogged,

I ran out of ambition, motivation,

I was creating, no yes there was creation,

Of frivolity and not loyalty,

Creation of room decor and a room as clean as my new notebooks,

I lacked the ability to think I'd go back to the dynamic I was,

I lacked the ambition to go back to the dynamic I was,

Couldn't sit at a table, nor could I stop thinking of how I could sit at a table,

It's funny how mere months of Merry and become a habit and you can't go back to what you were how much ever you desire,

No, perseverance and big mouthed terms don't seal the deal,

Forwardly thinking; there's isn't no deal,

There's isn't any going back when torpor becomes a habit,

There's isn't not going back when scrolling and clicking is the only worldly hobbit,

So that's where the stop to the binging must start,

But I lacked the ambition,

So empty were my submissions,

The past, proud bit of the pre lockdown was nothing but memories of omission,

And no, this didn't change with a singular caption on 'comment down below your suggestions on how I can regain lost bounds',

No a bunch of motivational videos won't enlighten,

So one thing I learnt if I learnt anything at all was,

When you lack,

You start over,

When there's nothing,

You make your own opening assets.

SECTION 9

Yearnings And Learnings

The Baffling Boy

The little boy, born late to odd parents, old parents,

Playing with ball, every action ever so transparent,

But beyond the actions lay emotions untold,

His story I couldn't fathom, couldn't unfold,

Little he was, belittled by his playmates,

It seemed as though his inverse universe was content and introspective,

Never expressing emotions, not even an antipodal perspective,

But as he played with the black ball, I saw color in his eyes,

This boy is strong, I inferred, the world he could suffice;

I saw a spark in him,

One that seemed far from dim,

He'd grow up to be big and lucrative,

He would never confide in a stranger's perspective,

For this child will run an empire,

Like one he's running inversely this moment,

Prepping the road for his delirium, he won't lament,

This boy isn't indifferent and yet he fits in,

This boy is an underdog who will always win.

Riches And Rags

INSIGHT

What are the rich? What are the poor? Who creates bounds and lines? How are they different? The bold line in our society between its two prominent sections is getting broader by the day. But if life is truly, in ever idealistic sense, about goodwill, then why does this line even exist? What does it seek? If at the end of the day, we die as one, why can't we live as one? Does death and remorse look at money and riches of people and personalities?

You understand that riches and rags are finally going to fade, right?

For once we're stubbed under the same soil, your satin slippers and my feet will both smell like fertilizer,

You know my tombstone will be grey, just as yours, right?

Worms will decompose us both and none will decipher,

You're moneyed, I'm not; the land won't bother,

For the land is loyal to none, just like you aren't;

I don't judge you because you're rich, brother,

But you judge me to be scant,

Therefore, I scorn at you,

Your riches bother me, they do,

And all your tries to make the mass feel blue,

But I bring solace to my raging soul,

By saying, "no matter of pride, no matter of legacies,

Burial is common to the quaint and the foul,"

I seldom attain joy, but this is one of my ecstasies.

City Lights In Small Eyes

INSIGHT

The fire in their belly, the heady twinkle in their eyes, the ambition in their heads... There's so much I can say about the deprived. Those who haven't seen cities, those who-haven't been born in privileged households, those who lack confidence and have come here to find it. The city and its small possessions fascinate them, amaze them. What's normal for us, isn't so for them. They tug onto every exposure, cease every opportunity, bring out their showman.

The yellow lights, the Empire State,

Questioning why I'm here, doubting its fate,

Girls of twenty-one,

Tanning under the sun,

Cherubic years long gone,

Legacies and legislatures here are born,

The immensity of the city matching with my eyes,

A shove and a push,

It comes to my mind; little girl in a big city,

Little girl won't seek no pity,

Lights flicker and so do careers in the big city,

So grow don't go little one, don't digress,

Everything is noted, a foul word turns into a transgress,

Grow little girl don't go,

Morph your emotions and mould them into elation,

Don't expect riches, face deprivation,

Small girl, big world,

Little girl big city,

Bring out the showman, stop being all giddy.

Guarded Ages

You're going to be what you dreamt of, I assure,

If not, everyone will end up doing something, I'm sure,

So be your age, enjoy phases,

Embrace crazes,

Ruined friendships aren't a benefactor,

Enjoy your oldest house, its every sector,

Enjoy the undrunk, drunk nights,

Enjoy the quandary of fights,

Seek success, it's what I say too,

But don't make that desire your journey,

Your journey are the neurotic friends you'll meet,

Sometimes you'll end up in jail,

They'll be there to get through a bail,

Your journey is the music, that changes as you do,

Times of rapture and ones that make you blue,

Seek success but joy is what brings it,

Enjoy your finite age to its every bit.

Words

The power to stain,

The power to gain,

The power to know,

The power to show,

They all come with wisdom,

They're knowledge's kingdom,

The knowledge with curbs,

This leads to suburbs,

The knowledge for right,

We use this to fight,

The kin of law,

Has more than a flaw,

All this comes with words;

For one who can't say,

For one who can't claim,

That one who can't blame,

That one with some shame,

Has no words to express,

Has no words to impress,

Has no thoughts to name.

SECTION -10

Fun And Frolic - Teenage Aches

Moods

Chafing fleshes,

Revelling spirits,

Rebelling, jumping hearts,

Shadows upon a dreamy day,

Heat of the sun ebbing my way,

Moods change like night and day,

Until at the quantum leap,

I finally decay.

Delhi

Delhi, you baffle me,

Leave me speechless,

Far from the elation of Innisfree,

Pollution and population quantify you Delhi,

The toxicity of teens,

Seldom found life and cheap greens,

Phones work their magic,

Rooftops are cool, not tragic,

Rape and crime; sinister and formidable,

From every caged bird to the crow on the loose cable,

Half of you is bold and sinful,

The other half bold and beautiful,

The maulvi roaming about Jama, captivates me,

The criminal on the loose, captures me,

You're divided, Delhi;

Townhalled for some and gullied Delhi-6 for others,

Birds roam free, but with clipped feathers,

The south of you, Disguising literacy,

The west of with unshielded illiteracy,

The Cantt and it's Scooty shenanigans,

Emporio to Gol Gappa bhaiyyas' ambitions,

Delhi you leave me perplexed,

Dark and light in one frame, it's complexed,

So here's to you being a trap yet liberated and free,

So here's to me discovering you and in the process, discovering me.

The Mighty Future

I hope you realize that it gets past the likes you got,

It goes beyond the diet you sought,

It gets bolder than that hashtag challenge you accepted,

It is way more quantified than the impression you reflected,

It is tougher than the math problem you cried over,

There is much more than that love bug which at the
moment hovers,

Thrills will come and no not only from the rooftop smokes,

Life is stored in much more than what at present it stokes,

It lays in the first full sunset,

Your self bought golf set,

The claps go beyond your school hall,

The last gown you'll mourn over won't be at a scanty ball,

So take it easy and let go of the loss you think is big,

For its nothing but a memory you missed making but instead you'll make it gold later.

Wait and Hold on to the memories that are already gold.

Being Lonely //
The Desire To Be Alone

There's always a time we long company,

We're sepulchral,

It all seems cruel,

We go out and cycle alone, looking at the group of kids chitter more, cycle less,

Longing to be like them,

Longing to be them,

If need be then,

Pitying every pedal we take,

Thinking how each pedal wouldn't matter if there were someone to pedal with,

Thinking how much louder you'd be cackling,

How much louder than the flock of loud folk,

Then you meet a bird of the flock, you tag along,

Join the flock,

You're finally one of them, you laugh, find pulchritude in their ever so messed up jokes,

You laugh so they don't launder you too,

Now there's another one of your old clan, looking at you, in hope to be like you one day, in hope to be you one day,

And as you cycle with the ever so shining flock,

The lonesome days perish and all you remember is the time you were garlanded into the clan,

Fondly, not fondly,

You just remember it,

But as you cackle louder, languidly become the king pin of the set,

You realise why the old leader left,

There's not much here,

It lacks true substance,

There's no prudence you're securing here,

It just gets worse, kings change faster, kings long to leave, subordinates stab and the hierarchy changes spot all over again,

Until the pair of envious eyes which cycled alone, merrily join the cackling clan,

Just like your initial envious plan,

And all you want now is for him to come and you to go,

You're envious of the him now,

You want to ride the cycle alone,

You want to rediscover the places you discovered; only this time alone,

Now you know that won't be loneliness, just solitude,

Just when you never thought you'd want to get away from people and just be alone,

All you want is a lonely way up a hill,

A lonely trip to nowhere,

To rethink and reiterate,

To place a finger on what you became and call it childhood; to grow and actually learn,

There was nothing in the clan, there was nothing in that flock,

And now when you're back, from your little sojourn into Neverland,

You cycle alone, wave at the flock,

With their new king; the envious boy who first looked to be you, he's finally got what he wanted,

You wave at them,

You see them,

And no, you don't long to be them,

You're happy cycling alone,

The sun shines and so do you,

The only roots you're watering are the ones in Neverland, where you go occasionally,

To rethink and reiterate,

To place a finger on what you are now,

And one day,

In Neverland, where you go occasionally,

You meet the envious boy turned king;

He's not king anymore,

He's ready to cycle alone,

"There's nothing left in the clan" he said

Your eyes approved, a sense of satisfaction crept in.

Of Popularity And Pleasing

Likes and comments, texts and stories,

Puffs and pictures on high high storeys,

Hyping people up, forgetting your own story,

Doing what they do, unrealistic and flowery,

Saying what you don't mean,

Seeing what you've never seen,

Pleasing the popular, forgetting the real ones,

Both please alike; daughters and sons,

Doing what you know is wrong and Formidable,

Thinking following followed trends is commendable,

Saying things that hurt,

For coolness you just blurt and blurt,

Forgetting your roots, losing your true nature,

Thinking doing what they do will make you Mature.

And slowly you're a new person,

Not better, just new,

So before life becomes a mere confession page,

Pause, rethink, know your age,

For Slowly, slowly you become them,

Toxic people, tugging onto a toxic hem.

Allusive Likings

I love like a forceful party,

Yes, my love is like a party,

Little games to ridicule boredom,

Little ways to strangle and get freedom,

Less physicalities, more formalities,

Sly innuendos and no sensualities,

Just wit and grit,

Fights to test your intellect,

Books to question your dialect,

No sugar, just salt,

Opening Every door you may bolt,

Rocks along the way,

I love like a hike,

With moods and mood spikes,

Love as forceful as small talk,

I love like a short walk,

A sojourn into fantasies of teenage,

Snapping out of sweetness, morphing into rage,

I love differently, it's almost preternatural,

But trust me fellow, my love is actual.

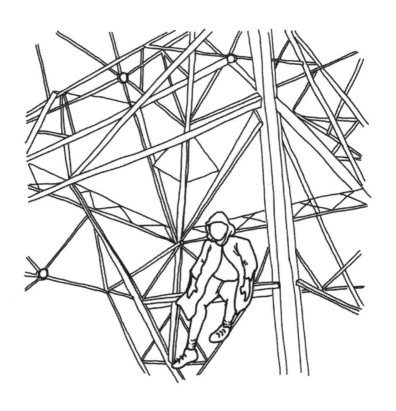

SECTION 11

Frostings –
The Short And Sweet Pieces

Brat

INSIGHT

Most of us grew up in bliss. Unaware and pampered. This is a light poem which I wrote as I scrolled through my childhood album. We were all such brats. We grew up too fast and now we miss the good ol' days...where it all seemed so easy. Where each tantrum we threw came off as nothing but a cute childlike quality. But all of that is only good up to a certain age. As old as I sound, we need to let go of our childhood habits one day or another. If not, it can cause some serious trauma and even drama! This poem is short yet is trying to convey the repercussions of sustaining your inner childhood brat. This poem is an emotion of fear; fear that introspects and asks, 'Am I still the same brat I was?'; 'Have I not become mature at all?' Maturity comes with age and wisdom for most. But what about those you gain age but no wisdom. What are we to do with a manchild?

I grew on childhood like lichen on wood,

Then the wood became me,

And I couldn't scrape the moss off,

Maturity never occurred,

Only childhood sustained,

The wood decayed.

Short And Sweet

INSIGHT

This poem is very deceptive. One has to read it again and again to actually understand it. Would you believe me if I told you this poem is about life and people? Yes, it is. In life there are people who are stern in their outlook and only get along with 'their type' of people. Then there are people who change for others. They're adjusting; for the good or for the bad, that depends, on the company one keeps, on the people one hangs out with; friends old and new; yet they change and adjust. In this poem, I talk of how someone is quite the opposite of who I am; they're harmful and not 'my type' of a person. But little did I know that that is only a pre-judgement. Sometimes people are deceptive and sometimes we judge people too fast. Little did I know that the person could in fact be a great friend. Little did I know how adjusting they would be. This poem is a lesson on not judging beforehand and also on how deceptive life and people can be; how sour and sweet life and people are!

You were candy and I was diabetic,

But little did I know you'd

become sour patch

for a man with cavities.

Art And Artistry

INSIGHT

Inspired by the quintessential way of living and life revolving around tea in India, a short and sweet anecdote into the life of every Indian and the essentiality of tea and how easily it's stirred up, just like emotions... Stirred and dissolved... A poetic analysis of tea and life and its fears and fatalities. This poem has a meaning deeper than what seems apparent. It also talks of how we are so scared you will acknowledge our fears, that we hide them; and in essence, gulp them down. Take everything with 'a pinch of salt.' Because of the constant stigma and terror of society, we are told to not come out with fears and with time it has subconsciously settled in our heads that the best way is to gulp it down. Silence isn't key in such matters but we make it essential to be quiet. We hush our fears so that we look strong. Acknowledging our fears is an art, thus I named the poem; art and artistry.

Heat the pot,

Pour the milk,

Gulp the fear,

Problem solved, my dear.

Made in the USA
Columbia, SC
11 December 2021

51035019R00131